8 STEPS TO FREEDOM

Breaking Free from the Inside Out:
A Guide to Mental, Spiritual, and
Physical Freedom

I0095755

Ruby J. Joyner

WWW.TRUEVINEPUBLISHING.ORG

8 Steps to Freedom
Ruby J. Joyner

Published by
True Vine Publishing Co.
810 Dominican Dr.
Nashville, TN 37228
www.TrueVinePublishing.org

Printed in the United States of America—First printing.

TABLE OF CONTENTS

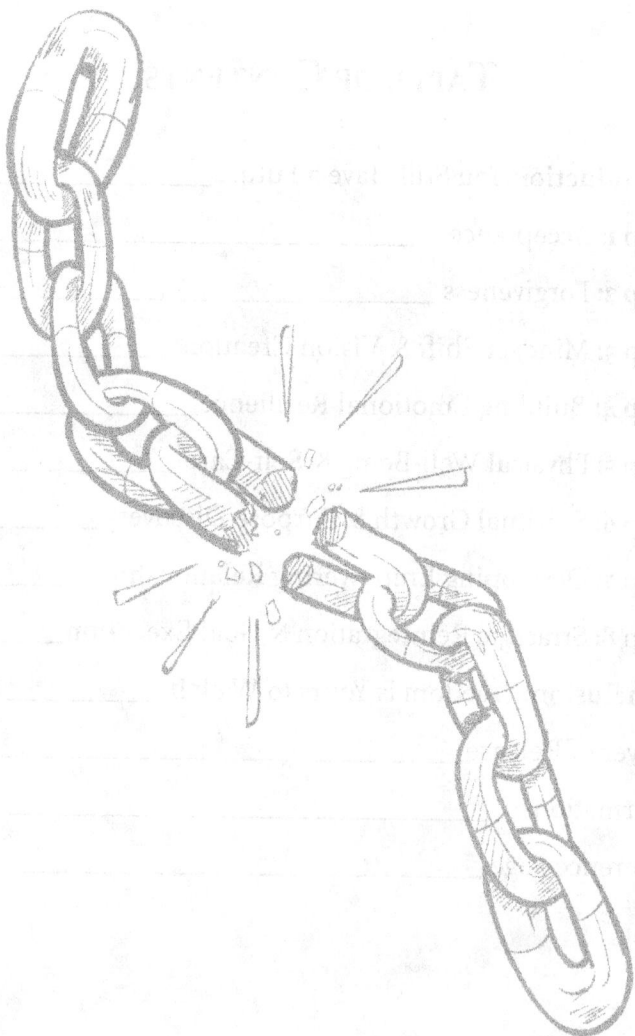

INTRODUCTION

YOU STILL HAVE A FUTURE

If you're reading this, I want you to know something right from the start: you are not beyond redemption. I don't care what's on your record, how many times you've been counted out, or how dark your past may seem—you still have a future.

My name is Ruby J. Joyner, and I've spent over 20 years working inside correctional facilities. I've walked the halls. I've looked into the eyes of men and women who feel forgotten. I've heard the stories, the regrets, the survival tactics, and the buried dreams. And I've seen the difference between someone who gives up and someone who decides to grow—right where they are.

I wrote *8 Steps to Freedom* because I've watched too many young women fall victim to trauma, poverty, and misguided beliefs that lead them into cycles of incarceration. I've seen brilliant minds buried under emotional pain, spiritual confusion, and hopelessness. I've also seen resilience rise in places no one expected it to. This book is my offering to every person behind bars who is ready to get free—not just on the outside, but from the inside out.

This isn't just a collection of lessons from a corrections official—it's a lifeline. These pages come from my years of listening, learning, and witnessing change. I've seen inmates mentor others. I've seen mothers fight for their children. I've seen men and women, hardened by trauma, find healing and soften through purpose. I've seen people who were once labeled as broken or dangerous become living proof that transformation is possible.

8 Steps to Freedom is not a list of theories. It's practical. It's spiritual. It's personal. It's built for people who want to get free—and stay free. Not just from a jail cell, but from the mindset, relationships, patterns, and pain that have kept them bound for too long.

Real freedom doesn't begin when the doors open— it begins when the mind shifts. It begins when you say, *"I want more. I was made for more."* You don't have to be perfect. You don't have to have all the answers. You just have to be willing. You need a plan. You need to believe— maybe for the first time in a long time—that it's not too late.

So read slowly. Let the words reach the parts of you that have been ignored or silenced. Highlight them. Wrestle with them. But whatever you do—don't walk away unchanged. Because somewhere inside you is the version of yourself you've been fighting to become. This book is your next step toward that version.

Let's walk it together. One page at a time.

Your freedom starts now.
— Ruby J. Joyner

Chief of Corrections, Davidson County Sheriff's Office, Leader, Believer in Second Chances, Advocate for Inner Freedom

STEP 1

ACCEPTANCE

The Doorway to Healing and Ownership

Freedom starts with accepting where you are while believing in where you can go.

The first step to total physical, spiritual, and emotional freedom is *acceptance*—acceptance that what has happened in your life has happened, and that no amount of guilt, regret, or replaying the moment will reverse it.

The anger, the frustration, the guilt, or the shame we carry doesn't change the past. It doesn't undo the pain. Still, we hold on to these emotional shackles as if they're the keys to the freedom we're desperate for.

Some of us try to ignore the emotions. **Some of us have tried medicating the pain away.**

We've tried being strong. We've tried pretending we weren't hurt.

We're not angry—we just "don't tolerate disrespect."

We're not bitter—we just "keep it real."

We rewrite the past in our minds, hoping the pain will shrink if we ignore it long enough.

But now we're here—tired, honest, and finally ready. And this is where everything changes.

Not because the past disappears, but because we stop running from it. We face it. We accept it for what it is, for what it did in our lives—and most importantly, we *release it* and *let it go.*

The Truth About Acceptance

Acceptance is often mistaken for weakness or giving up. But real acceptance is the opposite. It's choosing to stop wrestling with a version of the past that can't be rewritten, so you can finally write the future you deserve.

It's the moment you stop asking, *"Why did this happen to me?"* and start asking, *"What can I build from here?"*

Helen Keller's life is a powerful reminder of what happens when you stop asking, "Why did this happen to me?" and start asking, "What can I build from here?"

At just 19 months old, Helen became completely blind, deaf, and mute due to a severe illness. She was trapped in a world of silence and darkness, unable to see, hear, or speak. For many, that would have marked the end of possibility. She could have spent her life asking, "Why me?"—why did this happen, why was she different, why was life so unfair?

But Helen made a different choice. She decided that her limitations would not define her. Instead of mourning what she had lost, she leaned into what she had left—her mind, her will, and her determination to connect with the world.

She learned to read, write, and eventually speak. She became the first deaf-blind person to graduate from college, going on to write books, deliver speeches, and advocate for others living with disabilities. Helen Keller didn't regain her sight, hearing, or voice in the traditional sense—but she discovered a deeper voice within herself, one strong enough to inspire the world. Her life proves that even in the most impossible circumstances, when you stop reliving the pain and start building a purpose, nothing can stop you.

Now, we're not naïve. Acceptance doesn't instantly erase pain, scars, or memories. Some wounds run deep— they shape how we see ourselves, how we love, how we trust.

We build walls.

We live in survival mode.

We numb the pain with substances, performance, anger, silence, or perfectionism.

We try to outwork the wound instead of healing it.

But healing doesn't come from pretending.

Healing begins the moment you say:

"Yes, this happened. Yes, it hurt. But it no longer owns me."

Mya Angelo said, "I can be changed by what happens to me. But I refuse to be reduced by it."

Acceptance is radical because it demands honesty *and* compassion. It allows you to separate what happened *to* you from who you *are*.

And in that separation, you find your power:
To choose again.
To believe again.
To create again.
To live free.

What Acceptance Really Means

Acceptance doesn't mean you liked what happened. It doesn't mean you deserved it, invited it, or should have "known better." It means you've stopped running from the truth long enough to hold it in your hands and say, *"This is part of my story, but it's not the whole story."*

Your story is expanding in all directions. There are limitless possibilities and opportunities waiting for the person who is willing to let go of the past and explore the vastness of potential. When we avoid acceptance, we get stuck—replaying events, rehearsing pain, or blaming ourselves and others. But here's the truth: you can't change what you refuse to face. And you can't create the future while living in the shadow of the past.

Dave Dahl grew up in Oregon and made a lot of bad choices when he was younger. He got involved with drugs and crime, and ended up going to prison several times. He spent over 15 years behind bars for things like stealing and selling drugs. Life seemed like it would never change for him.

But everything started to shift when Dave decided to face his mistakes instead of running from them. While in prison, he joined a program that helped him recover from drug addiction and learn new skills. He took classes in design and computer work—and he got really good at it. Dave even started helping teach others, which gave him a sense of purpose.

When he got out of prison in 2004, he went back to his family's small bakery. This time, he wanted to do something different. He used what he had learned and came up with a special bread recipe. People loved it. That bread, which he called "Dave's Killer Bread," became a huge success. But even more inspiring? Dave hired other people who had also been in prison and needed a second chance.

Dave's life teaches us something powerful: **You can't change what you won't face, and you can't build a better future while holding onto a painful past.** Once Dave accepted his past, he was free to build a future filled with purpose, success, and hope—not just for himself, but for others too.

When you accept and release the people and decisions that caused your life hurt and pain, and decide to move on, you literally break chains that keep you bound and free yourself to experience a greater life.

Accepting Responsibility

"It's Not My Fault."Four simple words. But together, they form the sentence that keeps more people stuck than any trauma, tragedy, or trial ever could.

At just 27 years old, Demarco found himself facing three homicide charges. From the moment of his arrest, he pleaded his case: *"I didn't do anything. I was just the driver! It's not my fault!"*

But the courtroom didn't care about explanations. The jury didn't hear his desperation. After a long and grueling trial, Demarco was sentenced to 15 years behind bars. His denial couldn't save him from the weight of the law—or from the reality of his choices.

Too often we think that avoiding responsibility will shield us from pain, consequences, or accountability. But it does the opposite. It keeps us powerless. Vulnerable. Stuck.

When we say "It's not my fault," we may be right—but we also give away our right to grow. Holding yourself responsible for your role in any situation, no matter the context, empowers you to make better life decisions and learn from everything you endure in life.

Halfway through his sentence, something in Demarco broke... or maybe it began to heal. Tired of the cycle, tired of blaming everyone but himself, Demarco turned his heart toward a power greater than his own understanding. He started searching for purpose, for clarity, for truth.

From his cold, dank cell, he began to rehearse a different future. He'd close his eyes and picture the old crew pulling up, windows down, music blasting, asking him to ride one more time—to "hit a lick." But in his mind, he practiced a new response. One that took courage. One that said, *No.*

He knew what waited for him on the outside. The same streets. The same temptations. Nothing out there had changed. So he had to.

Demarco decided to start living differently *before* freedom came. Because if he couldn't stand strong behind bars, he'd never survive the pressure waiting on the other side.

Let's be clear: Taking responsibility doesn't mean blaming yourself for everything that happened to you. You are not at fault for being abused. You are not to blame for being neglected, abandoned, mistreated, or overlooked. You are not responsible for the injustice that wounded you.

But you *are* responsible for what you do now.

You are responsible for the thoughts you rehearse every morning. For the choices you make today. For the healing you're brave enough to pursue, and for the future you're bold enough to create.

Responsibility is not a burden—it's a key. A turning point. A declaration that says: "I'm no longer waiting to be rescued. I'm rising to rebuild."

Because freedom isn't found in blaming the past. It's found in accepting responsibility for your future.

"Our destiny is not written for us but by us"– Barak Obama

Steps to Acceptance:

Step One: Name the Pain

What we don't name, we can't heal. Write it down. Say it out loud. Whisper it in prayer. Let the truth come up, not to shame you, but to *free* you. You don't have to perform strength—you only need to be honest.

Reflection Prompt:

What experience or moment have I been trying to forget or outrun? What am I afraid will happen if I face it?

_____

_____

_____

_____

Step Two: Release the Blame

This part is hard. Blame, whether toward others or ourselves, is a shield we use to protect our pain. But true freedom comes when you let it go. This doesn't mean excusing anyone's actions. It means choosing to stop giving them power over your peace.

Reflection Prompt:

Who or what am I still blaming? What am I ready to release so I can take my power back?

_____

_____

_____

_____

Step Three: Embrace Compassion

You did the best you could with what you knew, felt, and had at the time. Acceptance blooms when you treat yourself with the kindness you would offer a child who's been hurt. You're still here. That in itself is a testimony.

Reflection Prompt:

If I spoke to myself like someone I love, what would I say right now?

_____

_____

_____

_____

Step Four: Own Your Next Chapter

This is the shift. This is where healing meets purpose. When you accept the past, you stop fighting for a different yesterday—and start building a better tomorrow. This is where you say, _"That was the chapter that shaped me. But it will not be the one that defines me."_

Ownership doesn't require perfection. It requires permission—permission to start again. To decide what kind of life you want to live from this point forward. When you take ownership of your future, you move from being a survivor to being a _creator_.

You stop asking for permission to heal, to grow, to shine. You begin walking in alignment with who you were always meant to be—whole, worthy, powerful.

"Happiness is when what you think, what you say, and what you do are in harmony." Mahatma Gandhi

Reflection Prompt:

If my past no longer held me back, what kind of future would I create? What would I dare to believe is possible for me?

_____

_____

_____

_____

The person you see in the mirror (reflection) and the person people get to see are not always the same. It's "introspection" time. What are the messages behind your reflection? Where did those messages come from?

_____

_____

_____

_____

Taking Ownership

You are not what you survived. You are what you do with it. This chapter may have started with acceptance, but it doesn't end there; after acceptance comes ownership.

Ownership is strength.

Ownership is not just about accepting responsibility—it's about claiming power. True strength is found when you stop blaming others for where you are and start *deciding* where you want to go– no matter how hard it will be or how long it will take to reach your destination. That shift changes everything. It turns setbacks into lessons, pain into purpose, and uncertainty into direction.

Owning your life means facing your reality without excuse and recognizing your power to create the reality you desire and change your life. That is strength. Anyone can point fingers. It takes real courage to say, *"This is mine to change."*

When you take ownership, you stop waiting for permission, approval, or rescue. You stop waiting for opposition and obstacles to move. You stop living in reaction to the past and start creating a future. Even small decisions—like showing up, setting boundaries, or choosing peace—become acts of strength because they come from a place of personal authority.

Ownership gives you clarity.

When you stop blaming others or waiting for perfect conditions, your vision becomes sharper. You begin to see what's really happening around you—and inside you.

Taking ownership strips away confusion because it forces you to face the truth: your choices matter. You're no longer drifting. You're deciding. And in that decision, things that once felt overwhelming start to make sense.

As you take responsibility for your actions, thoughts, and responses, patterns begin to reveal themselves. You start to notice what triggers you, what fuels you, and what drains you. You recognize cycles—both healthy and harmful—and gain the power to break or build them. With that awareness comes opportunity. You no longer feel like life is just happening to you; instead, you realize you have the ability to shape your direction by setting clear intentions.

This clarity leads to purpose-driven movement. You may not be able to control every situation, but you control how you show up in it. You choose your mindset, your attitude, and your actions. That's the beginning of real transformation—not because everything around you changes instantly, but because *you* do. And when you change, your life begins to shift in response. Ownership is the lens that sharpens your focus, the anchor that grounds you, and the key that unlocks the next level of your growth.

The strongest people aren't those who've had it easy. They're the ones who took what happened and built something better with it. They didn't let bitterness win. They turned wounds into wisdom and pain into purpose.

Ownership does not mean you will be perfect. Your decisions will not always be the correct decisions, and you

RUBY J. JOYNER

will not exercise your ownership 100% of the time, but it's about being present and powerful in your own life. And the moment you choose it—really choose it—you step into a strength that no one can take from you.

Ownership is a choice.

It takes determination to take ownership of your life. It is a choice. It not always easy. Taking ownership will feel lonely and uncertain, and it does not always give you the advantage. You must choose ownership of your life, no matter what.. Every time you decide to get back up after a fall, to speak your truth when it's easier to stay silent, or to keep going when quitting feels more comfortable, you're making a powerful decision. You are choosing to take your power back from fear, doubt, and outside control. Ownership doesn't require perfection—it only asks for your presence and your willingness to act.

When you choose ownership, you shift from being a victim of life to being the author of it. You no longer let your past, your circumstances, or the opinions of others define you, instead ownership is the quiet, consistent choice to keep showing up for yourself, even when no one else does.

Every act of ownership builds strength. With each decision to rise, you reinforce the truth that your life belongs to you. And the more you practice that choice, the more confident, resilient, and clear you become. You begin to trust yourself. You recognize that while you can't control everything, you can control you—and that power is what creates lasting change.

Ownership is control.

Ownership happens the moment you stop waiting for someone else to fix it, change it, or make it right—and you decide to take the lead in your own life. Control isn't about manipulating every outcome; it's about knowing that your choices, your mindset, and your actions are fully yours. When you take ownership, you stop handing over the steering wheel of your life to circumstances, people, or emotions. You reclaim the authority to guide your direction.

Owning your thoughts, habits, and behavior gives you the ability to respond instead of react. You begin to recognize that while you can't always control what happens *to* you, you can always control what happens *through* you. This creates internal stability. You become less shaken by what's outside because you're rooted in what's inside: self-awareness, self-discipline, and clarity. That kind of control doesn't limit you—it frees you.

Real control comes from within. It's not about forcing life to cooperate, but about staying grounded and intentional regardless of what life throws at you. Ownership allows you to set boundaries, make wise decisions, and move with confidence. It turns chaos into clarity and gives you the calm assurance that, no matter what, you're equipped to handle what comes next. Control through ownership is not power over others—it's power over *yourself*, and that's the most valuable kind there is.

It's time to take ownership of your life. Whether you are incarcerated mentally, physically, or spiritually. You're not voiceless. You have something to say, even if your voice shakes at first. You're not powerless. Every decision you make is a step toward the life you want. You're not broken. You are rebuilding—stronger and wiser.

Determine today, that you will no longer let your past, other people, or fear decide where you go next. Stand up and say, *"I get to decide my tomorrow."* The world may not change overnight—but if you have spoken those words, *you* are already changing. One choice at a time.

You don't need to be perfect to move forward. You just need to be willing. Healing is not about having all the answers. It's about choosing to take one more step, even when the road is hard. Even as an incarcerated person, you can still take ownership of your life. The quality of your life is not found in your location but in your mind. You will not always be bound to iron cells, scheduled recreation and chow times, so take a breath. Release the shame. Stand in your truth, and write what comes next.

Take the first step of ownership by writing down the future you want

_____

_____

_____

_____

_____

_____

_____

_____

_____

_____

Affirmation for Acceptance and Ownership

I accept my past, not as my identity, but as my history.

I accept responsibility for my life as a power to control my future.

I release what I can no longer carry.

I give myself permission to heal, to grow, and to thrive.

I am not defined by what happened to me—I am defined by what I choose today.

I take ownership of my life.

I honor my strength, my softness, my survival, and my becoming.

I am still writing my story—and it will be powerful.

The "New Chapter" Letter

Before you close this chapter, write a letter to your *future self*. Picture the person who has fully accepted their past and taken bold ownership of their future. Who are they? How do they walk, speak, and show up in the world? What do they need you to know right now?

Let this letter be your bridge from where you are to where you're going.

And remember: Healing doesn't mean forgetting. It means finally being *free enough to move forward.*

_____

_____

_____

_____

_____

_____

_____

STEP 2

FORGIVENESS

Nelson Mandela was a man who changed the world, not just through his leadership, but through his incredible decision to forgive. He spent 27 years in prison in South Africa because he stood up against a government that treated people unfairly based on the color of their skin. He was locked away, separated from his family, and forced to live in a small, cold prison cell. He had every reason to be angry, bitter, and full of hate.

But Mandela made a different choice. Even though the government had taken so much from him, he refused to let them take his heart or his peace. He once said, *"As I walked out the door toward the gate that would lead to my freedom, I knew if I didn't leave my bitterness and hatred behind, I'd still be in prison."* That's what forgiveness looks like. It's choosing peace for yourself, even when others don't deserve it.

When Mandela was finally released in 1990, many people expected him to seek revenge. But instead, he forgave the same people who had locked him up. He even worked with some of them to help bring peace to the country. His forgiveness helped bring an end to apartheid—the system of racial separation and unfair treatment—and led South Africa into a new season of unity and hope.

His choice to forgive didn't just heal his own heart—it healed a nation. If Mandela had stayed angry, South Africa might have fallen into more violence and pain. But because he let go of hate, he opened the door for peace, freedom, and respect between people of all races. In 1994, Mandela was elected the first Black president of South Africa. He became a symbol of strength, peace, and forgiveness for the entire world.

Nelson Mandela's story reminds us that forgiveness is not weakness—it's power. It takes strength to let go of anger and choose love. His life shows that even after years of pain and injustice, healing is possible. Forgiveness isn't always easy, but it can change everything.

Forgive Others

Unforgiveness is like drinking poison and hoping it will hurt the other person. But it doesn't. It only harms you. When someone hurts you, it's natural to feel pain, anger, or betrayal. But holding on to those feelings for too long can begin to damage your heart, your mind, and even your health.

Forgiveness isn't about pretending something didn't happen. It's about setting *yourself* free from the pain of the past so you can live in peace. When you hold on to anger, it becomes heavy. It affects the way you think, the way you speak, and even how you treat others. You may start to feel bitter, lose trust, or have trouble sleeping or focusing.

That's because the pain stays alive inside of you. But when you forgive, you allow healing to begin. Forgiveness doesn't mean the other person was right. It means you are choosing not to carry the hurt anymore.

When you choose to forgive, you take the power from the person who harmed you. Yes—*they have power over you* because whether you realize it or not, the person you're holding anger against still has a grip on your mind and emotions. That anger is like a chain connecting you to them, even if they're no longer in your life. And if they hurt you on purpose? Then your unforgiveness is doing exactly what they wanted—it's keeping their harm alive inside of you.

Think about how your mood changes when you remember someone who wronged you. Maybe your heart starts beating faster. Your chest feels tight. Your stomach twists into a knot. That's not just emotion—it's your body reacting to anger.

When you're angry, your brain sends signals to release chemicals like adrenaline and cortisol. These chemicals are part of your body's "fight or flight" response, which helps you react quickly when you're in danger. But when you stay angry for a long time, those same chemicals keep pumping through your body—and that's not healthy. Too much anger can lead to headaches, high blood pressure, stomach pain, and even trouble sleeping or focusing.

So when you hold on to anger, you're not punishing the other person. You're punishing yourself. Every time you replay the hurt in your mind, your body goes through the stress all over again. Even if they've moved on, disappeared, or even passed away, your pain is still doing the work *they started*. Your unforgiveness becomes a tool in their hands—even without them being present. You're helping their plan stay in motion by replaying the hurt over and over again.

Forgiveness doesn't mean what they did was okay. It doesn't let them off the hook—it lets *you* off the hook. It breaks the connection that lets their actions still affect your life today. When you forgive, you're saying, *"You no longer have access to my peace, my mind, or my future."*

When you think about the person, you no longer lose control of your emotions and allow harmful biological hormones to course through your body, harming you mentally and physically, but you are free to move forward with positive creative energy. You no longer internalize their mistreatment as a personal issue, but you realize their mistreatment of you is/was a reflection of their own shortcomings. You can walk in the confidence of knowing that you are more than what you have endured, and greater than your suffering. When you choose to forgive, you stop that cycle. You give your heart and body a chance to rest. You start to feel lighter, calmer, and more in control.

Forgiveness of Unintended Offenses

Sometimes, we hold on to anger and pain from things others said or did, but they may have no idea we were offended. While we're staying upset, replaying the moment in our heads, they're going on with their lives like nothing happened. In these cases, unforgiveness doesn't hurt them—it hurts *you*. You're carrying a weight that they don't even know exists.

When you don't forgive, it can cloud your thinking. Unforgiveness makes it hard to see the situation clearly. It can make you feel like everyone is against you, even when they're not. A small misunderstanding can grow into a big wall between you and someone who actually cares about you. The longer you hold on to it, the more it affects how you think and how you treat others—sometimes even people who had nothing to do with the original hurt.

Not everyone who hurts you does it on purpose. Sometimes people say things the wrong way or act out of their own pain. You might have friends or family members who offended you without realizing it. But when you choose not to forgive them, you push them away—even though they may have wanted to make it right. This can ruin good relationships that could have been saved with one honest conversation.

Forgiveness doesn't mean pretending it didn't hurt. It means deciding to give the other person the benefit of the doubt—and giving *yourself* peace. When you let go of the grudge, you open the door to healing, understanding, and stronger connections. Instead of living guarded and angry, you give yourself permission to be free, to think clearly, and to love deeply again.

Forgive Yourself

"Why do I need to forgive myself?" That's a good question—and an important one. A lot of people walk around feeling heavy, not because of what others did to them, but because of what *they* did to themselves. Maybe it was a choice you regret, something you said that hurt someone, or a chance you missed. You think about it again and again. You might even say you've moved on—but deep down, you haven't. That's why you need to forgive yourself.

We all make mistakes. No one is perfect. But when we hold on to guilt or shame, it's like carrying around a backpack full of rocks. Every memory, every "I should've done better," adds more weight. Over time, it wears you down. You might start to believe you don't deserve happiness or peace. That's not true. Everyone deserves a chance to grow and move forward—including you.

Forgiving yourself is different from pretending the mistake didn't happen. It's not saying, "It didn't matter," or "It was okay." Forgiveness means saying, "Yes, I messed up—but I've learned from it, and I won't let it define me." It's admitting the truth, then choosing to grow. That's a powerful thing to do.

Sometimes we're harder on ourselves than we are on anyone else. If your friend made the same mistake, you'd probably encourage them. You'd say, "It's okay, you're human. Learn from it." But when it's *you*, the voice in your head sounds mean and unforgiving. Why is that? Why is it so hard to give yourself the same kindness you give to others?

You may think staying angry at yourself will somehow make up for what you did. But it doesn't. It only keeps you stuck. You can't move forward if you're always looking back. The longer you carry guilt, the more it affects your mental and emotional health. You might feel sad, anxious, or even worthless. But you're not worthless—you're just holding on to pain that it's time to let go of.

Think of it this way: your past doesn't define you—your *choices* do. When you choose to forgive yourself, you're saying, "I know I've made mistakes, but I'm choosing to grow, to change, and to love myself anyway." That's not weakness. That's strength.

Many people, even adults, struggle with this. Take a look at stories from people who turned their lives around after hard times. Some were once in jail, on drugs, or hurting the people they loved. But at some point, they decided they didn't want to live like that anymore. They took responsibility, made better choices, and most of all—they forgave themselves. That's when true healing began.

Forgiving yourself might take time. It might not happen overnight. But you can start by being honest.

The Self-Forgiveness Challenge

What are you blaming yourself for? What do you keep replaying in your mind? Write it down. Say it out loud. Then ask yourself: *What can I learn from this? How can I grow from it?* Growth is a part of forgiveness.

Take time to identify mistakes, choices, and decisions you regret and still hang over your head. Change your perspective from viewing them as regrets and view them as lessons. In this exercise, you will write down the regret and the beneficial lesson you learned. Then you will say aloud, "I forgive myself for __(regret)_____ and I am grateful that from it, I learned _(lesson)___

Regret   Lesson

_____   _____

_____   _____

_____   _____

_____   _____

You're not the same person you were when the mistake happened. You've grown. You've changed. Don't judge your past self by what your present self now knows. That's not fair. Forgiveness means looking back with grace and moving forward with hope.

If you believe in God, you may find comfort in knowing that He offers forgiveness freely. The Bible says in 1 John 1:9, *"If we confess our sins, He is faithful and just to forgive us our sins and to cleanse us from all unrighteousness."* If God can forgive you, you can forgive yourself, too.

You're not the sum of your mistakes. You're the person who's learning, healing, and becoming better every day. So let go of the guilt. Drop the backpack full of shame.

Forgive yourself—not because you've forgotten, but because you're ready to live free.

How to Forgive

"I don't even know how to forgive. I have lived with anger and hatred so long. I have been told all of my life that I should never let anyone disrespect me. What does forgiveness even look like?"

If you've grown up hearing that respect is everything and that anger is power, it can feel confusing to even *want* to forgive. Forgiveness might sound like letting someone win or ignoring what they did. But that's not what forgiveness is. Forgiveness isn't saying what they did was okay—it's saying *you're not going to let it control you anymore.*

One person who had to learn the power of forgiveness is **Oprah Winfrey**. She grew up in poverty and faced terrible abuse as a child. She was mistreated by people who were supposed to protect her. For a long time, she carried that pain. But as she got older, she realized that holding on to anger was keeping her from living in peace. She once said, *"Forgiveness is giving up the hope that the past could have been any different."*

Oprah didn't say that lightly. She worked through years of hurt and trauma. But she chose to forgive—not just to set others free, but to set *herself* free. She knew that as long as she held on to the pain, it would still have power over her. By forgiving, she was able to heal and grow. She became one of the most successful and influential women in the world—not because she had no pain, but because she learned how to move beyond it.

So, what does forgiveness look like? The first and simplest way to forgive is to articulate the words.

Say it out loud:

"I forgive him/her." Say the name of the person and what they did.

"I forgive John, the school bully, for punching me in the face and embarrassing me in school."

Saying who you forgive, acknowledging what they did, and forgiving them verbally creates a new reality–one in which you take control of the narrative. You may have to say it multiple times for days, weeks, months, or years until it takes hold, but the simple act takes the power from the offense and puts it back in your hands.

Forgiveness looks like choosing peace over revenge. It means letting go of the need to "get even" and deciding that your mental and emotional peace matters more than proving a point. Revenge might feel satisfying in the moment, but it often leaves you feeling empty, unsatisfied, just as hurt—or worse—after it's done. Peace, on the other hand, allows you to move forward without the weight of anger dragging you down. When you choose peace, you're saying, *"I deserve to heal more than I deserve to stay mad."*

Your process of forgiveness might be writing down your feelings, talking to someone you trust, or praying for the strength to let go. It won't always feel good right away. But over time, your heart will start to feel lighter.

Forgiveness is not weakness

You might worry that forgiveness makes you look weak or soft. But it's the opposite. Forgiveness takes strength. It means you are strong enough to face your pain and strong enough to rise above it. You're not pretending nothing happened. You're choosing not to let it rule your life anymore.

Think about it this way: anger keeps you chained to the past. Forgiveness sets you free. You don't forgive people because they deserve it—you forgive because *you* deserve peace. Holding on to pain doesn't protect you. It only makes the wound stay open. Forgiveness helps it heal.

You might not know how to forgive yet. That's okay. Forgiveness is a process, and it starts with one decision: the decision to *try*.

The Healing Power of Forgiveness

Healing and forgiveness go hand in hand. You cannot truly heal if you are still holding on to anger, pain, or bitterness. When you hold on to those feelings, it's like carrying a heavy backpack everywhere you go. It wears you out, even if you don't realize it. Forgiveness is the key that opens the door to peace. Forgiveness helps you take the first real step toward healing.

When you forgive, your body and mind both benefit. Holding onto anger causes stress, and stress can lead to health problems like high blood pressure, trouble sleeping, and anxiety. But when you forgive, your body can begin to relax and recover. A study by Johns Hopkins University showed that people who forgive others have lower heart rates, lower blood pressure, and less risk of depression. This proves that forgiveness doesn't just feel good—it's also good for your health.

Forgiveness is powerful because it helps you let go of pain that has been holding you back. Maybe you've been hurt by a friend, a family member, or even yourself. That hurt builds walls around your heart. But when you forgive, those walls begin to fall. You stop reliving the hurt over and over, and you begin to make space for peace, love, and joy. You start to see life differently—not just through pain, but through growth and hope.

Forgiveness is a gift you give to your future. It helps you take control of your life again. You no longer live stuck in what happened—you begin to live in what *can* happen. Forgiveness doesn't change the past, but it *does* change your future. And that change starts with three powerful words: I Forgive You!

Take a few quiet minutes to think about these questions. Write from your heart—there are no wrong answers.

1. What is something someone did that hurt me and I'm still holding on to it?

Write what happened and how it made you feel.

_____

_____

_____

_____

2. How has holding on to this hurt affected me—emotionally, mentally, or physically?

Example: Do you get angry easily? Do you feel tired, stressed, or distracted?

_____

_____

_____

_____

3. What would it feel like to let this go?

Try to picture your life without the weight of that pain.

_____

_____

_____

_____

4. Is there someone I need to forgive—or do I need to forgive myself? Why?

_____

_____

_____

_____

5. What is one small step I can take toward healing today?

It could be writing a letter you don't send, saying a prayer, or just admitting how you really feel.

_____

_____

_____

_____

Affirmation to Remember:

"Forgiveness doesn't change the past, but it opens the door to peace in the future."

MINDSET SHIFT & VISION CREATION

Before he became one of the most powerful voices of his time, Malcolm X was just another inmate. He was locked up at 20 years old—angry, bitter, and full of questions. In his early days behind bars, he used to argue with guards, waste time, and look for fights. But something started to change. A fellow inmate challenged him to stop blaming the system and start using his time to educate himself. At first, Malcolm resisted. But eventually, he picked up a book. Then another. He started copying the dictionary word by word, teaching himself how to read and write better. That discipline became the start of a new life.

Years later, Malcolm said that prison was where he became truly free. Not because the gates opened, but because his mind did.

Freedom doesn't begin the day you're released. It begins the moment you decide to think differently. You may be behind bars, but your mind can still be free. You can create a future worth walking into—but it starts with your mindset and your vision.

Right now, you might feel ashamed. Angry. Hopeless. You might be worried that no one believes in you, or even that you're not sure you believe in yourself. Those are real feelings. But you don't have to let them rule your story. You are not your past. You are not your mistakes. You are a human being with the ability to grow, change, and rise.

One of the most important steps in this journey is your mindset shift. A mindset is simply the way you think about yourself and the world. If your thoughts are filled with shame, guilt, and fear, it will hold you down. But if you begin to shift those thoughts toward purpose, growth, and hope, you can lift yourself out—starting from the inside.

But here's a question you must wrestle with: **How long shall we wallow in negativity?** How long shall we allow the same destructive thoughts to cycle through our minds and dictate the road we travel on? Every time you accept a lie as truth, you give it power. You surrender the steering wheel of your life.

In the quietness of our minds, we allow negative messages to have dominion over us. *Dominion* is a big word. It means "sovereign or supreme authority; the power of governing and controlling." Think about that. Are your thoughts governing you—or are you governing them?

A young man once said, "I can't do nothing but sell drugs. In my community, that's ALL a broke n***a can do to feed his family." *LIES.*

Another young woman said, "The most valuable thing I have to offer is my body... I'm not giving it away for free." *SELF-DESTRUCTIVE.*

These are not just words. These are declarations that shape behavior, identity, and destiny. Can you identify the impact of such messages in your own life? Can you identify thoughts that have had **dominion** over you? Who or what has been governing your mind?

EXERCISE 1: THOUGHT CHECK

Write down five negative things you've said or thought about yourself. Then, next to each one, write a truth to replace it. Example:

"I always mess up." → "I've made mistakes, but I'm learning to do better."

_____

_____

_____

_____

The more often you replace negative thoughts with empowering ones, the more your mindset begins to shift.

Vision

Vision is a clear picture of the life you want to build. Even if you're locked up, even if you have years left to serve, you still need a vision. Why? Because vision gives your pain a purpose. It gives your choices direction. Without vision, you're just surviving. With vision, you're building.

Imagine this. You're 10 years from now. You're free— not just physically, but mentally, emotionally, and spiritually. What does your life look like? Where are you? Who's around you? What are you doing every day?

Don't just imagine money or stuff. Think about how you want to *feel*. Do you want to feel peace? Purpose? Stability? Dignity?

That's your vision trying to speak to you.

There was a man I met in a correctional workshop who used to say, "I'm already free. I just haven't gone home yet." He woke up each morning with purpose. He tutored other inmates. He led a small group. He even wrote a business plan from inside his cell. Years later, he opened a small repair shop. But freedom for him started before the release. It started with his vision.

EXERCISE 2: FUTURE YOU LETTER

Write a letter to yourself from the future—10 years ahead. In this letter, describe the kind of person you've become. What kind of relationships do you have? How do you think? How do you handle stress? What have you overcome?

Start like this:

"Dear Me,

I want you to know that you made it. You didn't give up. I'm proud of you for..."

Be as detailed as you can. This letter becomes a mirror of the life you're building.

There are messages that will lead to **self-imposed bondage.** The belief that you'll never change. The lie that you're only good at breaking the law. The whisper that you're not worthy of love or success. But freedom doesn't come by accident. **Embracing a new way of thinking leads to freedom.** And that embrace requires **action.** It takes **courage** to tap into a new way of living—not by force, but by **choice.**

One of the lies that many incarcerated people believe is, "It's too late for me." That's not true. It's not too late to grow. Not too late to learn. Not too late to earn back trust. Not too late to become the kind of person even you can be proud of.

Shifting your mindset takes work. Creating vision takes courage. But if you're willing to do the work, you'll discover that your power never left—it just got buried under pain, mistakes, and fear.

So, how do you keep going when the walls close in? When your time feels heavy? When your past won't let go?

You build a system.

EXERCISE 3: DAILY FREEDOM ROUTINE

Every morning for the next 30 days, do this:

- ◆ Sit still and breathe deeply 5 times.
- ◆ Say at least 1 positive truth about yourself out loud.
- ◆ Read your Future You letter or vision notes.

47

- ◆ Write 1 thing you're grateful for.
- ◆ Write 1 thing you will do today to become that version of yourself.

Simple. Repeatable. Powerful. In 30 days, you'll notice a shift.

The Story of James

James was 19 when he was sentenced to 18 years for armed robbery. By his own words, he was "reckless, selfish, and angry at the world." For the first few years, he just survived—fights, time in the hole, and a growing list of write-ups. But one day, after hearing that his younger sister had dropped out of school, he broke down. He realized that his life had become a burden on the people who loved him.

That night, James wrote two words in a notebook: *"Start over."*

He started reading again. He enrolled in a GED class. He wrote letters to his sister, encouraging her to finish school. He stopped hanging around with guys who wanted trouble. It was slow, and it was hard. But over the next 5 years, James changed.

Today, he works at a reentry center. He helps people coming out of prison find housing, jobs, and peace of mind. James didn't just get out of prison—he got free in his mind long before his body ever walked out the gate.

If he could start over, you can too.

You may have been broken, but you are not beyond repair. You may have made some bad decisions, but you still have time to make new ones. Your life is not over. It's just under construction.

Your thoughts matter. Your vision matters. Your choices today are building your tomorrow. Every book you read, every class you take, every apology you make, every truth you speak to yourself—they all count. Even in the dark, seeds are growing.

So ask yourself again: How long shall we wallow in negativity? How long will you let lies, shame, and fear hold the key to your future?

It's not going to be easy. The road to mental and emotional freedom is filled with challenges. But it's also filled with reward. Peace. Clarity. Strength. Purpose. All of that is available to you.

You are not forgotten. You are not too far gone. You are not just a number. You are a person with the power to choose what kind of life you build from here on out.

Start today.

Change your thoughts.

Write your vision.

Walk in the direction of your future.

Even if you don't see it yet, it's already waiting for you.

Affirmation: *"I am not my past—I am my choice to change, my vision for the future, and my decision to begin again."*

BUILDING EMOTIONAL RESILIENCE

Learn to process emotions in a healthy way. Develop coping mechanisms that prevent setbacks and help navigate challenges with strength and wisdom.

Shaka Senghor was 19 years old when he was sentenced to 17 years in prison for second-degree murder. Like many others, he didn't plan to end up in prison. He was a young man dealing with pain, loss, and street life. He had built emotional walls just to survive. But inside those prison walls, Shaka stayed angry. He fought other inmates. He got sent to segregation. He didn't trust anybody.

"I didn't want to feel anything," he later said. "Feeling meant remembering. And remembering meant pain."

But everything started to change when he received a letter from the mother of the man he had killed. She told him she forgave him.

Shaka said that moment broke something inside of him—and opened the door to something new. He began to think about the pain he had caused others, and the pain he still carried inside himself. For the first time, he began to face it.

He started journaling. He read books about trauma and healing. He practiced managing his anger and emotions. Over time, he didn't just grow—he transformed.

Today, Shaka is a bestselling author, speaker, and mentor. He teaches people how to face their past, take control of their emotions, and change their lives.

What Is Emotional Resilience?

Emotional resilience is the ability to face pain, stress, and hard times—and still move forward. It means learning how to feel your emotions without letting them control you. It means building strength on the inside so you don't break on the outside.

In prison, emotional resilience is not just helpful—it's survival. You deal with grief, disrespect, betrayal, frustration, and fear. Some people explode. Others shut down completely. But neither reaction leads to healing.

You don't have to let your emotions run your life. You don't have to act like you don't feel anything, and you don't have to act like every feeling deserves a fight. **You can learn to feel and still have control.** That's emotional strength.

Let's look at what happens when emotions get trapped inside:

- **Anger turns into violence.**
- **Shame turns into self-hate.**
- **Fear turns into silence.**
- **Loneliness turns into desperation.**

When emotions are left unspoken and unprocessed, they don't just disappear—they grow heavier. Anger that stays locked inside eventually needs an outlet. For many, that outlet becomes violence, not always physical, but emotional, verbal, or internal. That anger turns into outbursts, conflicts, and sometimes even self-sabotage.

Shame is another silent weight. It whispers lies like, "You're not good enough" or "You'll never change," until that shame becomes self-hate. The more you believe these lies– that you are unworthy of love, respect, or even redemption– it will lead you to self-hate.

Fear, when unaddressed, silences your voice. It keeps you from speaking up, asking for help, or standing your ground. And loneliness—especially behind bars— can become a dangerous hunger. People start making desperate decisions just to feel connected or wanted. That desperation leads to toxic relationships, risky behavior, or emotional shutdown.

The truth is this: **when we don't deal with our emotions, they begin to deal with us.** They start shaping our choices, hijacking our peace, and pulling us back into the same painful cycles we swore we'd never repeat. That's why emotional resilience isn't just helpful—it's necessary for your freedom.

Is Walking Away a Weakness?

DeShawn was in line for chow when a guy bumped into him on purpose.

"Watch where you going," the guy barked.

DeShawn's chest got tight. His fists curled. His breathing sped up. He had two choices: blow up—or breathe.

"I counted in my head," he said. "I told myself, 'Don't let this dude cost you more time.' I walked away."

His hands were shaking, but his peace stayed intact.

Let's keep it real. In prison, walking away can make you a target. People might think you're weak. They might try to test you even more. That's the reality. So walking away isn't always easy—and it doesn't mean letting people run over you.

Walking away with strength is different from backing down in fear. You can walk away with your head high, your chest out, and your purpose clear. You don't have to entertain every challenge that comes your way.

Emotional resilience isn't about being soft. It's about being **smart**. You've got to think long-term. Say things like:

- ◆ "I'm focused right now. I'm not going back and forth."
- ◆ "You don't control me. I got too much on the line."

If you feel unsafe, speak up. Talk to a counselor, a chaplain, or someone in authority. Taking steps to protect your life and peace is not snitching—it's survival with strategy.

The strongest people aren't always the loudest. They're the ones who know how to choose their battles, control their emotions, and stay focused on freedom— real freedom, inside and out.

Three Tools to Build Emotional Resilience

1. Name It to Tame It

You can't deal with what you won't name. By identifying your emotion, you empower yourself to take control of it. When you feel something big, ask yourself: *What is this feeling really about?* Is it anger—or am I hurt? Am I quiet because I'm calm, or because I'm scared?

Naming the emotion doesn't make it go away, but it helps you stop it from controlling your next move. It creates a pause between what you feel and what you do. That pause is where your power lives. When you can name what's happening inside you, you shift from reacting out of habit to responding with intention. It's the first step in taking back ownership of your emotions—and your life.

2. Breathe Before You React

Your body gives you warning signs. Tight chest. Tension in your jaw. Clenched fists. That's your body saying, *Slow down.* This slows your heart rate, clears your head, and helps you think before you act.

Use this breathing pattern to reset:

4-4-4 Method:

- Breathe in for 4 seconds
- Hold for 4 seconds
- Breathe out for 4 seconds
- Repeat 4 times

3. Rewrite the Story in Your Mind

The way we experience life isn't just based on what happens—it's based on how we *interpret* what happens. Two people can go through the same situation and walk away with two totally different realities, simply because of the story they told themselves about it. This is why naming your emotions is so important.

When you don't stop to ask *"what am I really feeling?"*, your mind will make up a story—and often, it's the wrong one. You might tell yourself, "He disrespected me on purpose," when maybe he didn't even see you. You might say, "She's ignoring me because she hates me," when really she's dealing with her own grief.

The stories we tell ourselves can create connection or conflict. Peace or pain. Healing or destruction. But when you learn to name the emotion underneath the story—hurt, fear, jealousy, shame—you give yourself the power to change the meaning. And when you change the meaning, you change your reality.

AFFIRMATION:

"I am healing with wisdom, guiding my emotions with strength, and building a better me without losing my peace or dignity."

EXERCISE: EMOTION CHECK-IN

Each night for five days, write:

- One strong emotion you felt
- What triggered it
- How you responded
- How you wish you had responded

Example:

Emotion: Frustration

Trigger: Someone skipped me in line

Response: Snapped at them

Better response: Took a breath and kept calm

EXERCISE: THE TRIGGER TRACKER

Track your emotional triggers for one full week. Each day, write:

1. What upset you
2. How your body reacted
3. How you responded
4. What you'll do differently next time

This helps you spot patterns and make stronger choices in the moment.

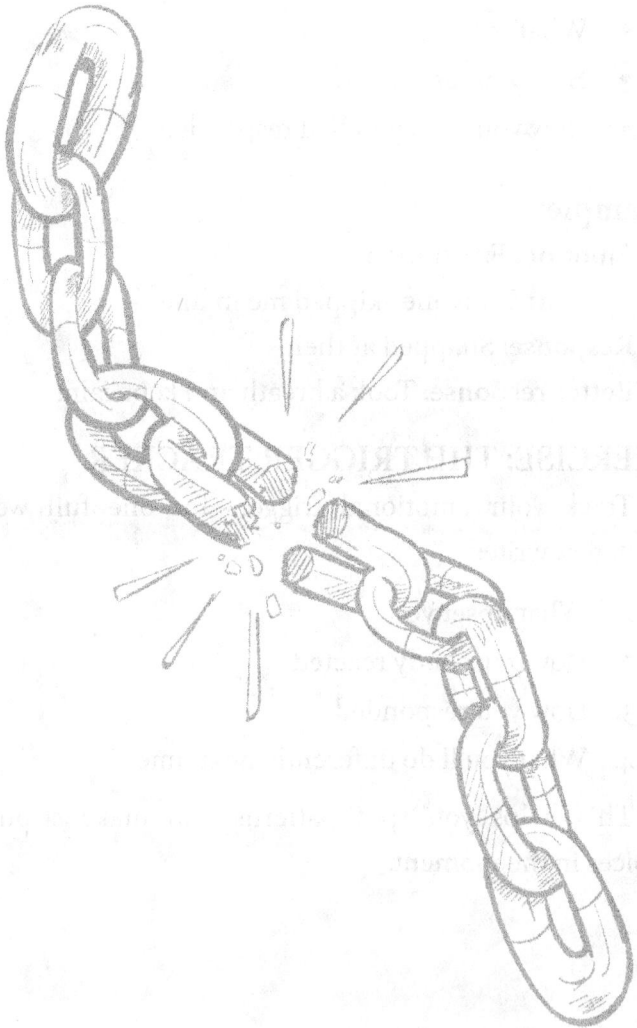

PHYSICAL WELL-BEING & SELF-CARE

Prioritize health through movement, proper nutrition, and self-care practices that enhance overall well-being and energy.

When Tupac Shakur was locked up in Clinton Correctional Facility in 1995, he was at a breaking point. Just 23 years old, he was already one of the most famous rappers in the world—but fame didn't protect him from pain. He was angry, betrayed, and tired. But inside that cold cell, something shifted.

He later shared in interviews that during his time in prison, he stopped drinking, stopped smoking, and started focusing on getting his body and mind right. "I had to face myself," he said. "No distractions. No friends. Just me, my thoughts, and God."

Each day, Tupac made time to read, write, and reflect. He did push-ups, sit-ups, and paced his cell to keep his blood moving. It wasn't about looking good—it was about feeling *alive* again. About regaining a sense of control.

The prison guards noticed the change. Other inmates did too. One officer said, "He moved like a man who had something to protect—his future."

You don't have to be a celebrity to make that same choice. Whether you're in a cell or just stuck in a cycle of unhealthy habits, you can reclaim your body—one step at a time. You don't need a gym. You need a decision. Small daily choices like movement, clean eating, and caring for yourself can unlock strength you didn't know you had. Freedom starts on the inside, and your body is a big part of that journey.

Your body is the one place you live every single day. If your mind is the driver, then your body is the vehicle. You wouldn't drive a car for years without changing the oil or filling the tank. But many of us try to live our lives on empty. When we ignore our physical health, everything else suffers. We become tired, emotionally drained, and mentally foggy. Even our spirit feels distant. That's why it's so important to pay attention to how we care for ourselves.

Let's start with the first major area: movement.

Movement That Frees You

You don't need a gym to move your body. You don't need a trainer, a treadmill, or a new outfit. What you need is a made-up mind and a commitment to begin where you are. Movement is not about how you look—it's about how you feel. It's about reclaiming your strength, your breath, and your sense of power.

Even five minutes of movement a day can start to shift your energy. Jumping jacks, push-ups, walking in place, stretching—these small acts activate your muscles and get your blood flowing. If you start your morning with light movement, you may notice your mood lift and your mind clear. If you wind down your day with stretching, you might sleep better.

Here is a simple daily practice you can do:

Morning Routine: Start with 20 jumping jacks, 10 push-ups (or wall push-ups), 20 high knees, 10 squats, and a 30-second full-body stretch.

Evening Routine: Take 30 seconds to breathe deeply, do slow neck rolls, seated toe touches, 10 slow leg lifts on each side, and a 1-minute full-body stretch.

These movements are not just physical; they are declarations. Every time you move your body, you remind yourself that you are alive and you still have power over your day.

Exercise Prompt: For seven days, commit to doing some form of movement for five minutes each day. Write down how you feel afterward. Circle the day you felt the strongest or most at peace.

Nutrition That Fuels You

You are what you eat. That isn't just a saying; it's a biological truth. Food is information. Each meal teaches your body what to do—whether to heal, inflame, energize, or drain you. In many prisons, food choices are limited, and healthy options aren't always accessible. But even with limitations, you still have choices.

Start by drinking more water. It sounds simple, but most people are more dehydrated than they realize. Water clears toxins, boosts energy, and even helps with focus.

RUBY J. JOYNER

Next, cut back on sugar and overly processed foods when you can. These foods often give you a quick high followed by a deep crash, leaving you more tired and irritable than before.

If fruits, vegetables, or whole grains are available to you, make those your priority. Eat slowly and mindfully. Try to notice how different foods make you feel. Do they energize you or leave you feeling sluggish? Awareness is the first step to better choices.

Mindful Eating Practice: At your next meal, take three deep breaths before your first bite. Chew slowly and focus on the taste, texture, and how full you feel as you eat. Don't rush. This builds discipline and helps your body digest more efficiently.

Think about the times you eat out of anger, sadness, or boredom. What are you really feeding in those moments? What are you hungry for?

Self-Care That Restores You

Self-care isn't selfish. It's a survival skill. In high-stress environments, especially in incarceration, your mental health is under constant attack. Creating routines that restore your peace is essential to staying centered.

Start with your space. A clean and organized environment can clear your mind. Make your bed. Fold your clothes. Wipe down surfaces. These small acts give a sense of order and control.

Next, care for your body with intention. Comb your hair, wash your face, and take care of your appearance.

These actions might seem small, but they send a powerful message to your brain: "I am worth taking care of."

Don't forget stillness. Sit for five minutes a day in silence. Focus on your breathing. This helps calm your nervous system and reduce anxiety. If you can, read something encouraging each day—a devotional, a poem, a scripture, or a short book that inspires you.

Emotional Check-In Practice: Once a day, ask yourself, "What do I feel right now?" Write down your answer in a journal. Don't judge your emotions. Just notice them.

Journaling Prompt: What is one small way I can show myself kindness today?

When You Feel Like Giving Up

There will be days when nothing feels worth it. Days when your body aches, your mind is tired, and your motivation is gone. On those days, the last thing you'll want to do is care for yourself.

But that's exactly when it matters most. You're not weak for feeling low. You're human. But remember this truth: your effort still counts.

Every push-up, every sip of water, every decision to get out of bed and show up for yourself is a step toward freedom. It may not feel like much in the moment, but over time it builds strength—mental, physical, and emotional.

As Tupac once said, "I changed in prison. I grew. I focused. I became sharper."

You can too.

Final Exercise: Design Your Personal Self-Care Plan

Creating a plan gives structure to your new habits. Use the table below to map out your week. Choose one simple movement, one nutrition goal, and one self-care practice for each day. Don't worry about perfection—just commit to consistency.

Day	Movement	Nutrition Goal	Self-Care Practice
Mon			
Tue			
Wed			
Thu			
Fri			
Sat			
Sun			

Print or draw this table and place it somewhere visible. Update it weekly as your habits grow stronger.

Freedom isn't just a goal. It's a lifestyle. And it begins with how you care for yourself each day. When you choose movement, you reject stagnation. When you choose nourishment, you reject self-destruction. When you choose self-care, you affirm your worth.

Your body is the house of your destiny. Protect it. Honor it. And most of all, love it.

Affirmation:

I honor my body as the foundation of my freedom, strength, and purpose.

SPIRITUAL GROWTH & PURPOSE DISCOVERY

At just sixteen years old, Cyntoia Brown-Long was arrested for killing a man who had picked her up while she was being exploited and traficked. She had been controlled and abused by an older man who manipulated her into dangerous and degrading situations.

The night of the killing, she acted out of fear and desperation. Despite her young age and the circumstances of her exploitation, Cyntoia was tried as an adult and sentenced to life in prison. Her case sparked national outrage as activists and celebrities shed light on the injustice of sentencing a teenage victim of sex traffiking to spend the rest of her life behind bars. But what happened during her time in prison was just as powerful as her legal fight.

Isolated and broken, Cyntoia began turning inward, seeking healing and answers from a deeper place. She connected to a divine presence—not through religion, but through stillness, reflection, and listening to her inner voice. Through that relationship with the infinite, she transformed her mindset and began to walk in purpose. She earned her GED, college degrees, and became an advocate for others caught in similar cycles. After serving 15 years, she was granted clemency in 2019. Cyntoia's story is a testament to the power of spiritual awakening, personal growth, and the freedom that begins within.

What Is Spiritual Growth?

Spiritual growth is about awakening. It's recognizing that within each of us is a divine spark that connects to an infinite source—one that is boundless in power, wisdom, and love–a source of inextinguishable; unchangeable light. This source goes by many names: God, Creator, Provider, and more. Trust in and connection to this source is paramount.

Spiritual growth happens when you realize you are not alone, even in your most isolated moment. Growing spiritually means understanding that God is in you and learning to trust the God inside of you. It means becoming aware of your divine nature and living in a way that reflects your sacred connection to everything around you.

Spiritual growth does not mean you are perfect—it means you are progressing. It's the ongoing journey of becoming more aware, more connected, and more intentional in how you live and love. True spiritual growth involves acknowledging your flaws, confronting your inner struggles, and learning from your experiences, not hiding them. It means being honest with yourself about where you are while remaining open to transformation.

Perfection is not the goal; alignment with your higher self and a deeper connection to the infinite creative source is. It's about striving for authenticity, not flawlessness—because growth is found in the process, not the pretense

How Do I Start?

Starting a spiritual journey begins with a willingness to slow down and listen—not to the noise around you, but to the quiet within. It requires giving yourself permission to just be quiet and absorb offerings with the inherent power to guide you toward connection to the greater Source.

The first step is to acknowledge that there is more to you than your body and your past. There is a deeper essence—your spirit—that is already connected to something infinite, something greater. Begin by creating a space for stillness each day. Whether it's five minutes before bed or while sitting outside, close your eyes, breathe deeply, and simply ask for guidance to awakening the divinity within. You may not hear a booming voice or see visions, but you'll start to feel nudges—moments of insight, peace, or clarity that come from within. Honor those.

Next, start documenting what you notice. Write down your thoughts, dreams, and questions, even if they don't make sense yet. Pay attention to what stirs your heart or brings you peace. These are clues. A spiritual journey is not a straight line; it's a deepening spiral inward, toward your most authentic self. Allow yourself to evolve, to release old beliefs that no longer serve you, and to be open to truth that resonates with your spirit.

Surround yourself with things that uplift your energy—nature, quiet moments, meaningful conversation. The journey won't be about reaching a destination but becoming more present and aligned with the divine truth already inside you.

Declare affirmative beliefs about who you are as a spiritual being whether mentally or verbally. Think or say "I Am" statements.

"I Am worthy"
"I Am one with the infinite power greater than myself"
"I Am capable"
"I AM FREE"

Lastly, express gratitude. Showing gratitude is an important part of growing spiritually. It helps you focus on the good things in your life instead of what you don't have. When you take time to be thankful, it opens your heart and helps you feel more calm and connected. Gratitude helps you see that even in hard times, there is still something good—like having people who care about you, learning from mistakes, or just being alive. As you grow spiritually, being thankful becomes a way of thinking, not just something you do once in a while. It helps you feel closer to yourself, to others, and to something greater than you.

Discovering Purpose Through the Infinite

Purpose is the special way you give back to the world. It's how you use your talents, ideas, and kindness to help others and make a difference. Purpose is not just about having a job or doing tasks—it's about the reason behind what you do. It's what gives your life meaning and helps you feel proud of how you live. Whether you help one person or many, your purpose is your chance to leave a positive mark and make the world a better place, just by being who you are and doing what you care about.

Purpose is not something we find by doing more. It's something we uncover by *being* more—more present, more conscious, more aligned with our inner being. Your purpose is the unique way your divine energy expresses itself in the world. It is not limited to titles, roles, or careers. It is how you heal, how you speak, how you create, how you love.

The more you connect to the infinite power greater yourself, the clearer your purpose becomes. It may come to you in the quiet—when you're journaling, walking, dreaming. It might rise up in emotion when you're deeply moved by someone else's story or in the desire to help someone else break free. These moments are not random—they're clues. Following them is how you walk in purpose. Cyntoia's purpose was not defined by her sentence, but revealed through her healing. Yours will be revealed through your awakening. And it will liberate you.

Your purpose is not confined by your location or circumstances—whether you are walking freely through city streets or sitting behind prison walls, your purpose remains active and alive. It is woven into your very being, operating through your thoughts, your words, your influence, and your resilience. Purpose doesn't wait for the perfect moment or setting; it shows up in how you treat others, how you persevere, and how you choose to grow in whatever space you occupy. Even in confinement, your purpose can inspire, uplift, create, and transform lives— including your own. The power of purpose transcends physical boundaries because it is rooted in who you are, not where you are.

How to discover your purpose

There are many paths to discovering your purpose, but one powerful equation to consider is:

G + P = P, (Gift + Passion = Purpose)

Your gift is the natural ability or talent you possess— something that comes easily to you and has the potential to impact others. Your passion is the thing that stirs your soul, fuels your enthusiasm, and gives you energy even when circumstances are tough. When you combine what you're naturally good at with what sets your heart on fire, you begin to walk in your true purpose. This alignment not only brings fulfillment but also creates meaningful impact, because your purpose is often found where your strengths meet your deepest sense of drive.

Let's discover your purpose.

What are your gifts? What are those skills, talents, or personality traits that come easily to you? Your gift is something that seems so easy to you, you probably believe everyone should be able to do it. In fact, you probably think to yourself, "why is this so difficult for them to understand?"

Gifts are not confined to singing, rapping, dancing, or athleticism. Gifts can be quick thinking, a willingness to address and resolve conflict, salesmanship, or even the ability to make people smile. Take time to really consider this question. Dig deep.

_____

_____

_____

_____

What is your passion? Passion is the thing that fills you with energy and excitement, that stirs something deep within you and makes time seem to stand still when you're engaged in it. Passion often reveals itself through strong emotions—whether it's the joy you feel when helping others, the fire that rises when you witness injustice, or the peace that comes from creating, teaching, or serving. It's what makes you feel truly alive and deeply connected to something greater than yourself. When you identify what consistently ignites that sense of purpose and fulfillment, you're likely standing face-to-face with your passion.

Note: Making money is not a passion. It's a desire. If you lived in a world where everything was free, you will not be passionate about making money. Furthermore, the desire for money is not about the money, it's about what the money can get you.

_____

_____

_____

_____

What is your purpose? Now that you've discovered your gift and passion, it's time to combine the two to see how they can be used to make a difference in the world.

For example, chef and humanitarian José Andrés has a gift for cooking and a passion for helping people in crisis. He combined the two to start World Central Kitchen, a nonprofit that provides meals to communities affected by natural disasters and conflict. By using his gift to serve his passion, he found his purpose—and changed countless lives along the way.

How can you combine your gift and passion to walk in your purpose?

I am gifted at: _____

I am passionate about: _____

_____

My Purpose is: _____

_____

Don't fixate on creating one specific purpose. A person can have multiple purposes in life, and that's completely normal. As you grow, learn, and experience different seasons, your purpose may shift or expand. You might find purpose in raising a family, serving your community, starting a business, mentoring others, or using your creativity to inspire change.

Each stage of life can bring new opportunities to use your gifts and passions in different ways. Having more than one purpose doesn't mean you're confused—it means you're growing. Life is full of chapters, and each one may reveal a new way you're meant to contribute to the world.

Activate Your Divine Connection

1. Stillness Practice – Sit quietly for five minutes. Breathe deeply. Ask your higher self: What do I need to hear today? Don't force the answer. Just listen.

2. Write to The Infinite Power – Begin with 'Dear Infinite Creator...' and write a letter about what you desire, fear, or hope. Don't edit. Let it flow. Then read it aloud.

3. Follow the Spark – Each day, notice when you feel a tug on your spirit. It might be when you see someone in pain, when you get an idea, or when you feel drawn to speak. That spark is your spirit leading. Act on it.

4. Affirmation Work – Stand in front of a mirror or go to a secluded location and affirm your greatness: Example:

'I am a divine spirit. I am deeply connected to infinite love. I trust the wisdom within me.' I Am Love, I Am Peace, I Am Forgiven. I Am Free. Add as many positive "I Am" affirmations as you can think of.

Affirmation

I am becoming. I am not lost—I am awakening. My spirit is divine, my voice is sacred, and my life is guided by God - the power greater than myself."

DEVELOPING EMPOWERING RELATIONSHIPS –

When Curtis "Wall Street" Carroll first picked up a financial section of the newspaper, he had no idea it would change his life. He was incarcerated at San Quentin State Prison, serving a sentence for robbery and murder—locked up at just 17 years old. The fluorescent lights buzzed overhead, and the clang of gates echoed through the unit. He wasn't looking for a miracle that day—just something to read. But when he asked a prison volunteer what the tiny numbers in the paper meant, she told him they were stock prices. Curtis was stunned.

"I thought only rich people understood that stuff," he later recalled in an interview.

But that was the seed. And that seed was watered—not just by his curiosity, but by the people he allowed into his life. Mentors from outside the prison, educators, other inmates who were committed to transformation—all became his support system. And that system became his strategy for success. Curtis didn't just find information—he found people who believed he was worth investing in.

This is what empowering relationships do. They don't just cheer you on—they challenge you. They don't remind you of your past—they point you to your potential. And when you're rebuilding your life, especially after years of pain, trauma, incarceration, or addiction, the people around you matter more than ever. The right ones can be a lifeline. The wrong ones can be an anchor. Freedom isn't just about leaving a cell. It's about surrounding yourself with voices that remind you you're more than your worst mistake.

Curtis didn't have a father figure growing up. He learned to read in prison. But he found mentors—people who challenged his thinking, showed him love through accountability, and gave him space to grow without judgment. In one interview, he shared how the relationships he built inside and outside of San Quentin became his foundation. "They taught me how to think," he said. "They didn't just give me information—they gave me tools to change my life." One volunteer even challenged him directly, saying, "You've got all this knowledge, but what are you doing with it?" That confrontation sparked what would become the Financial Literacy Program inside San Quentin. Curtis didn't keep what he learned to himself—he used it to empower others. That's the cycle of freedom: healed people help people heal.

A Bad friend is your worst enemy

A bad friend is your worst enemy because they don't come at you with obvious harm—they come cloaked in trust. Unlike a clear enemy, who you expect to betray or attack you, a bad friend gains access to your heart, your plans, your weaknesses, and your dreams. And because you let them in close, they have the power to influence your decisions, shape your mindset, and sometimes even derail your destiny. A bad friend will cosign your foolishness, lie to keep you comfortable, and smile while watching you fail. They won't challenge you when you're wrong or cheer you on when you're trying to grow. Instead of pushing you forward, they hold you in the past. They may laugh with you but never build with you. And that kind of relationship—one that looks like loyalty but rots from the inside—is more dangerous than any known enemy. Why? Because you won't see the damage coming until it's already done.

Now think about your circle. Who do you talk to the most? Who speaks into your life? There's a saying: *Show me your friends, and I'll show you your future.* If your five closest relationships are negative, stagnant, or unhealthy, your growth will suffer. But if they are positive, driven, honest, and supportive—you'll rise. You don't need perfect people. You need people with purpose. People who aren't afraid to speak truth with love. People who see beyond your scars and speak to your strength.

But let's be honest: letting go of unhealthy relationships can be hard. Especially if those people are familiar. Friends from the block. Cousins you ran with. People you love who just aren't ready to change. Sarah, a formerly incarcerated woman who now mentors other women reentering society, said it best: "Loyalty almost killed me. I had to learn that loving people from a distance doesn't mean I've turned my back—it means I'm protecting my purpose." She didn't cut people off out of hate. She simply stopped handing her growth to those who couldn't hold it.

That's what Curtis did too. He created boundaries without bitterness. He didn't argue with people who weren't ready. He just surrounded himself with those who were. "I didn't need cheerleaders," he said. "I needed coaches." There's a difference. Cheerleaders make noise. Coaches help you win. They correct you, encourage you, and hold you accountable. Who's coaching you right now? Who are you allowing into your most vulnerable spaces?

Identifying Empowering Relationships

Empowering relationships are built on five key traits that we call the perfect M.A.T.C.H. These qualities form the foundation of a circle that can help you thrive, not just survive.

M: Mutual growth means all parties seek the benefit of the others. Empowering relationships go both ways. You're not the only one benefiting from the relationship or giving to the relationshp—both people are helping each other grow. You're not always the student or always the teacher; you're both. When you're surrounded by people who are also doing their inner work, learning new things, breaking old habits, and moving toward purpose, it pushes you to rise higher. You sharpen each other. You inspire each other. That kind of energy multiplies progress.

A: Accountability is when someone cares enough to check on your progress, remind you of your goals, and hold you to the standard you set for yourself. They're not trying to control you—they're helping you stay on course.

It's the friend who says, "I know you're tired, but we didn't come this far to quit." Accountability isn't judgment. It's partnership. It's someone walking beside you and refusing to let you fall without a fight.

T: Trust is the soil everything else grows from. Without it, you're always second-guessing people's motives and guarding your heart. Trust doesn't happen overnight—it's earned over time. It's built through little things: someone keeping their word, showing up when they say they will, or simply listening without judgment. When you can trust someone, your walls come down. You stop living in defense mode and start letting love, truth, and healing in.

C: Consistency proves commitment. Anybody can show up once and say the right words, but it's the ones who keep showing up—week after week, call after call—that make a real difference. You need people who are steady, not seasonal. People who remember what you said last month and are still rooting for you today. Growth requires stability, and consistency creates safety. You can breathe easier when you know someone isn't going to disappear the moment things get rough.

H: Honesty keeps the relationship real. Surface-level connections don't help you grow. You need people who can tell you the truth even when it's uncomfortable. Someone who says, "You're not being real with yourself right now," can be more valuable than someone who only tells you what you want to hear. Honesty creates depth, and depth creates transformation. You don't need harsh critics—you need honest encouragers who care enough to keep it 100.

And don't forget: *you* are someone else's potential empowering relationship. What you're learning right now, someone else desperately needs. Maybe it's your child. Maybe it's your cellmate. Maybe it's a younger version of you, standing at a crossroads. When you become someone who lifts others up, you activate a different kind of freedom. A freedom that's not just for you—but flows through you.

How to find Good Relationships?

Finding the right circle starts with knowing what you need. Are you looking for encouragement, accountability, wisdom, or all of the above? Start by looking in places where people are already growing. That could be a recovery group, a reentry program, a church, a community class, or even a book club focused on self-development. Don't be afraid to ask questions and introduce yourself.

You're not looking for perfect people—you're looking for people with purpose. Watch how they treat others, how they talk when no one's watching, and whether their actions match their words. That's how trust begins: not with big promises, but with small, consistent actions.

Also, don't overlook people who are already around you but maybe haven't been fully invited into your growth journey. Sometimes a cousin, neighbor, or old friend is also trying to get better—but no one has said it out loud. Be brave enough to say, "Hey, I'm trying to grow and stay focused. You interested in doing this with me?" That one question can open the door to a powerful new connection. And remember: finding the right people might take time. Don't get discouraged if the first group or person isn't a good fit. Keep showing up, keep being real, and keep believing you're worth a circle that helps you rise.

EXERCISE: Find Your MATCH – Building Empowering Relationships

Your relationships can either build you or break you. Use the MATCH framework—**Mutual Growth, Accountability, Trust, Consistency, and Honesty**— to evaluate the people in your life and begin building a stronger, healthier circle of support.

Step 1: Identify Your Growth Needs

In what areas do you need help on your growth journey

_____

_____

_____

_____

Who do you know who embodies these qualities and can help you grow

_____

_____

_____

_____

Step 2. Relationship Reflection

List five people you currently interact with regularly (family, friends, mentors, cellmates, church members, etc.):

1. _____
2. _____
3. _____
4. _____
5. _____

Step 3: Evaluate the MATCH

For each person, ask yourself the following questions:

- Do we support **Mutual Growth**? Are they also trying to improve themselves?

- Is there **Accountability** in this relationship? Can we challenge each other respectfully?

- Do I **Trust** this person to keep it real and safe with my truth?

- Are they **Consistent,** or do they show up only when it benefits them?

- Can we be **Honest** without fear of judgment or fallout?

Put a ✓ next to each name for every MATCH trait that applies. Be honest with yourself.

Step 4: Identify What Needs to Shift

- Who in your life do you need to **spend less time with** because they no longer match your growth?

_____

- Who in your life do you want to **invest more time in** because they reflect where you're headed?

_____

- Is there someone new you want to reach out to (mentor, support group, family member)?

_____

Step 5: Set Your 30-Day Relationship Goal

In the next 30 days, I will:

☐ Join a support group or positive community (church, nonprofit, program)

☐ Have a real conversation with someone about accountability or trust

☐ Let go of one toxic or distracting connection

☐ Reach out to someone who inspires me and ask for guidance

☐ Strengthen a current relationship by showing up more consistently

You can check more than one. Make a plan and follow through.

Affirmation

I am surrounded by people who believe in my purpose. I welcome relationships that nourish my growth and release those that hinder my freedom. I am worthy of healthy, empowering connections.

STEP 8

STRATEGIC REINTEGRATION & GOAL EXECUTION

Plan for life beyond imprisonment by setting realistic goals, learning new skills, and preparing for a successful reentry into society with confidence and direction.

When Jesse Crosson stepped outside the prison gates after serving nearly 19 years, he didn't feel instantly free—he felt overwhelmed. The sky stretched wide above him, unfamiliar sounds buzzed around him, and even the weight of his own clothes felt strange. He was holding a small bag with a few belongings, but emotionally he was carrying the pressure of beginning a brand-new life. "I felt like I had a second chance," he later shared, "but I didn't know how to live it yet." There was no cheering crowd. No job waiting. No instruction manual. Just a man, a little hope, and a blank page.

That blank page is where many people give up. But Jesse made a decision that would change everything: *to treat reentry like a mission.* He didn't try to do everything at once. He started small. Each morning, he made his bed. He went on walks to clear his head. He made a list of goals for the day, no matter how small—apply for ID, go to a recovery meeting, learn how to use the GPS on his phone. These simple actions gave structure to the chaos of freedom. Over time, the daily discipline became a foundation. The foundation became a routine. And the routine became a new life.

That's what strategic reintegration looks like. It's not about trying to be perfect overnight. It's about planning your next steps with purpose and walking them out with discipline. Being released from prison is only the beginning. If you don't have a vision for your life, the world will give you distractions. Old habits. Old people. Old neighborhoods. But this step is your opportunity to decide what *you* want your life to look like. And then build toward it, one day at a time.

Jesse used journaling and social media to process and document his journey. "I wanted to show people what it really looks like to start over," he said. His posts were raw and real—him getting nervous in a grocery store aisle, fumbling with an ATM, or reflecting on conversations with loved ones. But that vulnerability became a strength. People saw themselves in his struggle. More importantly, they saw his resilience. Today, Jesse runs the *Second Chancer Foundation* and travels the country advocating for justice reform and supporting people returning home. He turned his strategy into service.

Create A Plan

Transformation doesn't happen by accident. It happens with a plan. Whether you're weeks, months, or years from release—or already walking in your freedom—you need a strategy. Begin by setting goals in three categories:

- Short-term (30–90 days),
- Mid-term (3–6 months), and
- Long-term (6–12+ months).

Your short-term goals might include getting your birth certificate, securing housing, or finding a local support group. Mid-term goals may include completing a certification, saving $1,000, or improving your health. Long-term goals could look like owning a business, reconnecting with your children, or mentoring someone else walking the same road.

Setting goals is important, but goals by themselves won't get you anywhere. What really makes change happen are the daily actions you take—the habits you build and repeat. You don't need to figure out your whole future today. You don't need to know exactly how you'll reach every dream. You just need a system. A system is a set of simple, repeatable steps that keep you moving forward, even when motivation runs low or life gets hard.

Think of a man who wants to build muscle. He doesn't need to know every science behind nutrition or how muscles grow—he just needs to stick to the system: eat right, train daily, and rest. If he follows that plan, his body will change. It's the same with your freedom. If you follow a system of learning, working, showing up, and staying consistent, your life will change too. You don't have to be perfect. You just have to do the work. Over time, those small daily actions—waking up on time, setting goals, studying, applying—will create the future you're aiming for. The results are in the routine.

How to develop your system

Creating a system starts with identifying exactly what you want to accomplish. Be clear. Whether it's getting a job, starting a business, earning a certification, or simply staying clean and focused—you have to know your target. Once you know what you're aiming for, break it down into all the steps it will take to get there. Ask yourself: What has to happen first? What needs to happen after that? Next, figure out what resources or people you'll need to complete those steps. That could include mentors, classes, documents, equipment, or community support. Then, turn those steps into a daily plan. Assign each action a time and a place in your day. This becomes your routine—the repeatable part of your system. When you follow that routine consistently, your system goes to work for you. It removes guesswork, builds momentum, and brings your goals to life one step at a time.

Your system could be writing a to-do list each morning, setting a weekly check-in with a mentor, or blocking off time to apply for jobs and read. Jesse didn't just talk about what he wanted. He created small wins every day. That's how confidence is built—not in huge leaps, but in consistent action.

Build Your System for Success

A system is a set of repeatable actions that take the guesswork out of progress. Follow the steps below to build a system that works for your goal.

1. Identify the Goal

What is one specific goal you want to accomplish?

Example: Get a full-time job, start a business, stay sober, complete a course

My Goal:

_____

_____

2. Break It Down into Action Steps

What steps will it take to reach this goal? Think in order—from start to finish.

1. _____
2. _____
3. _____
4. _____
5. _____

3. Identify the People & Resources You Need

Who can help you? What tools, programs, or information do you need?

People (mentors, case workers, friends):

_____

Resources (classes, tools, internet access, etc.):

_____

_____

4. Build Your Daily Plan

What 2–3 things can you do *every day* to keep moving forward?

1. _____

2. _____

3. _____

4. _____

📅 *What time of day will you do them?*

5. Create Your Accountability System

Who will check in with you to make sure you're staying on track?

Name:_____

How often will you check in? (Daily, Weekly, etc.): ___

_____

Daily System Summary

Every day, I will:

☐ _____

☐ _____

☐ _____

I will follow this system for: ___ days/weeks, then review my progress.

Learn New Skills

Reentry also means stepping into a world that may look very different from the one you left. Technology, language, jobs, even the way people communicate—all of it may have changed. That can feel overwhelming at first, like the world moved on without you. But here's the truth: you can catch up, and in many ways, you can even get ahead. Growth doesn't belong to any one group. It belongs to those who are willing to learn. You don't need to know everything. You just need to start where you are and be open to the process. The sooner you begin, the stronger and more confident you'll feel about your next chapter.

Learning new skills is one of the smartest and most empowering moves you can make after incarceration. Whether it's barbering, welding, coding, culinary arts, or small business development—there are resources out there waiting for you. Many trade schools and local programs offer free or low-cost training specifically for people reentering society. Some even help you get your first tools or uniforms. YouTube, Khan Academy, Coursera, and other online platforms provide entire courses for free—right from your phone. And don't underestimate the value of life skills: learning how to communicate, manage time, and set boundaries are just as important as any technical training.

Local support can be just as valuable as national programs. Many workforce development centers offer help with building resumes, practicing for interviews, learning how to use computers, or applying for jobs online. Some churches and nonprofits offer reentry programs that include mentorship, personal development, and job placement. These are not handouts—they are stepping stones. Take advantage of what's available. There is no shame in asking for help or starting small. Everyone has to start somewhere. The difference between those who grow and those who stay stuck is simply the willingness to take the first step.

So don't wait around for someone to hand you an opportunity. Go create it. Ask questions. Walk into buildings. Pick up flyers. Call the number. Sign up for the class. Show up to the workshop. Watch the videos. Practice until it clicks. Learning is not about being perfect—it's about being consistent. Every skill you gain becomes another brick in the foundation of your new life. You're not just trying to get by—you're building a future. And learning is one of the most powerful tools you have to make that future real.

Guarding Your Environment

Another key part of reintegration is guarding your environment. Who you live with, where you spend time, and what energy you allow around you matters more than ever. It's easy to fall into survival mode and return to familiar places—but that's where many people lose their progress. Sometimes the most strategic move is creating distance from what's familiar in order to create room for what's possible. You don't owe anyone your downfall. You owe yourself a future.

Even the right goals won't stick if you're surrounded by the wrong energy. If you're trying to change but everyone around you is still living recklessly, it will wear you down. You'll either isolate or start slipping without even noticing. That's why your environment isn't just about location—it's about atmosphere. Ask yourself: Does this space give me peace or stress? Does this person help me grow or pull me back? If the answer makes you uncomfortable, that's your cue to make a shift. It's not disloyal to protect your progress. It's wise.

Sometimes guarding your environment means saying no to people you love. That's hard. You may have to draw boundaries with friends or family who still live in the lifestyle you're trying to leave behind. You may love them, but you can't let them be louder than your purpose. Growth requires space—space to think, heal, and rebuild. Don't let guilt or obligation make you stay where you're shrinking. Real love supports your transformation, even if it doesn't understand it at first.

You also have the power to create your own environment—even if it's just a corner of a room or a daily routine that grounds you. Create a space that feels like peace. Put up quotes, keep a notebook, play uplifting music, or wake up early before the noise starts. Build a mental environment of vision and hope. When your outside world is chaotic, your inner world must be calm and clear. Guarding your environment is more than protection—it's preparation for who you're becoming.

Staying Anchored

And finally, stay mentally and spiritually anchored. The journey after incarceration isn't always straight or smooth. There will be days when everything feels heavy—when your record blocks an opportunity, when people judge you without knowing your heart, or when you've worked hard but the progress feels slow. Those moments can shake your confidence. But you can't let them break your spirit. That's when you need to stay grounded in something deeper than circumstances. That's when you remind yourself that setbacks are part of the process, not the end of the story.

When the world starts speaking doubt, you have to speak life. Use your voice to shift your mindset. Say it out loud: *I am not who I was. I am who I am becoming.* Those words carry power. They cancel out shame and call forward your future. Your thoughts shape your direction. So feed your mind with truth—listen to positive messages, read things that inspire you, and surround yourself with people who remind you who you are. Even if no one else is cheering for you, you can still be your own encourager. Sometimes the strongest thing you can do is stand in front of a mirror and speak the future you believe in.

Part of staying anchored also means returning to your "why." Why are you doing this? Why did you decide to change? Why does your future matter? When you revisit your purpose, you recharge your drive. Whether it's for your children, your peace, your freedom, or your faith—keep that reason close. Write it down. Look at it every day. When your purpose is clear, your problems don't feel as powerful. Let your goals guide you. Let your future speak louder than your fears. Fear may still show up—but it doesn't have to lead.

Like Jesse Crosson, you don't have to have everything figured out. He didn't leave prison with a blueprint—he left with intention. He built his life one step, one post, one conversation at a time. You can do the same. The path won't be perfect, but it will be yours. Keep walking. Keep learning. Keep adjusting. Keep believing. Staying anchored doesn't mean you never wobble—it means you never drift so far that you forget who you're becoming. Your freedom is not just about what's behind you—it's about who you decide to be from this day forward.

EXERCISE: Reentry Roadmap – Your Strategic Plan

1. Define Your Vision

In one sentence, describe what success looks like for you one year from now:

_____

2. Short-Term Goals (30–90 Days)

• What do you need to feel stable and focused right now?

☐ ID / documentation
☐ Housing
☐ Support group / mentorship
☐ Recovery or spiritual group
☐ Daily routine / planner
→ Other: _____

3. Mid-Term Goals (3–6 Months)

• What new skills or experiences do you want?

☐ Trade certification
☐ Steady income
☐ Save $____
☐ Emotional healing
☐ Healthy routine
→ Other: _____

4. Long-Term Goals (6–12+ Months)

Where do you want to be a year from now?

☐ Independent housing

☐ Start a business

☐ Reunite with family

☐ Mentor someone else

→ Other: _____

5. Daily Actions

◆ What 3 small actions can you take *daily* to move forward?

→ 1. _____

→ 2. _____

→ 3. _____

6. Accountability

Who will you check in with weekly to stay focused?

→ _____

Post this plan somewhere visible. Review and revise it every week. Don't aim for perfect—aim for progress.

Affirmation

I am not just released—I am ready. I have a plan, a purpose, and the power to follow through. I choose to grow daily, move forward boldly, and build a life that reflects who I truly am.

FREEDOM IS YOURS TO WALK IN

You've made it to the end of this book—but this is not the end of your journey. In fact, it's only the beginning. The pages you've just read are more than information—they are invitation. An invitation to own your life, confront your past, and walk boldly into a future that reflects your worth.

In Step One, you learned the power of Acceptance and Ownership. You cannot change what you refuse to face. The first step toward real freedom is taking responsibility—not with shame, but with courage. Ownership gives you back your power. You are not a victim of your past—you are the author of what comes next.

In Step Two, we walked through Forgiveness—not just of others, but of yourself. Forgiveness is not forgetting. It's releasing. It's the act of saying, "I choose peace over pain." When you forgive, you create space for healing. You stop bleeding into your future what was broken in your past.

Step Three challenged you to make a Mindset Shift and begin Vision Creation. Freedom starts in your thoughts. You have the right to imagine a better life. You have the power to think beyond your surroundings and dream beyond your current circumstances. Every great transformation begins in the mind.

In Step Four, you were invited to build Emotional Resilience. Life will test you—but you don't have to break.

You now have tools to process your feelings, confront your triggers, and respond with wisdom instead of reaction. Resilience doesn't mean you don't feel—it means you don't fold.

Step Five reminded you to care for your body with Physical Wellbeing and Self-Care. This vessel carries your vision. How you treat it matters. Fuel it. Move it. Rest it. When you take care of your body, you're practicing love and discipline at the same time.

Then came Step Six—Spiritual Growth and Purpose Discovery. You're not here by accident. You have a divine spark within you. When you reconnect with God – your infinite power within, you tap into the wisdom, creativity, and peace that's been there all along. You were created on purpose—for purpose.

Step Seven helped you evaluate your relationships. Developing Empowering Relationships means surrounding yourself with people who water your growth, not drain it. You don't need a crowd—you need a circle that reflects your future, not your past.

And finally, Step Eight brought it all together with Strategic Reintegration and Goal Execution. Don't just dream—build. Plan your steps. Learn new skills. Stay consistent. Freedom without direction leads to frustration. But freedom with a plan? That leads to fulfillment.

So here you are—with tools in your hand and a fire in your chest. You don't have to wait to feel free. Freedom is not a place—it's a decision. It's a daily choice to show up, grow up, and speak life into yourself.

Now it's your turn.

To apply what you've learned.

To walk in who you're becoming.

To believe that you are already enough—and you're just getting started.

Your story isn't over.

Your freedom is not a fantasy.

It's real.

It's possible.

And it's yours.

Now go live it.

PRAYER OF RELEASE

God, I thank You for walking with me through every step of this journey. Through darkness and disappointment, through struggle and silence—You never left me.

Today, I release everything that no longer serves me.

I release the pain, the shame, the guilt, the fear, and the lies I once believed about myself.

I release the people, the habits, the thoughts, and the patterns that kept me bound.

I surrender every chain—seen and unseen.

I no longer live in survival mode. I choose to live in purpose.

I release the weight of regret and pick up the promise of redemption.

I am not who I was—I am who You are calling me to become.

God, give me the strength to keep going, the wisdom to make better choices, the courage to face myself with honesty, and the peace to know that I am already loved, already worthy, and already free.

Let Your Spirit guide me in every decision.

Let Your truth be louder than my fears.

And let Your grace go before me as I build the life You created me to live.

This is my release.

This is my freedom.

This is my new beginning.

AFFIRMATIONS:

Step	Affirmation
Step One: Acceptance and Ownership	I take full responsibility for my life and my growth begins with me.
Step Two: Forgiveness	I release the past and make room for peace. I forgive so I can be free.
Step Three: Mindset Shift and Vision Creation	My thoughts create my future. I choose to believe in what's possible.
Step Four: Building Emotional Resilience	I feel deeply, but I do not fold. I rise with wisdom, strength, and grace.
Step Five: Physical Wellbeing and Self-Care	My body is sacred. I honor it with care, movement, and nourishment.
Step Six: Spiritual Growth and Purpose	I am connected to a divine source. My purpose is within me and guiding me daily.
Step Seven: Developing Empowering Relationships	I attract relationships that reflect my growth and protect my peace.

Step Eight: Strategic Reintegration and Goal Execution	My plan has power. I take one step at a time and build the life I deserve.

REFERENCE PAGE

The Story of My Life by Helen Keller. Doubleday, 1903.

Dave's Killer Bread – Company history and founder biography, Dave Dahl. <u>https://www.daveskillerbread.com</u>

Maya Angelou. Quote: "I can be changed by what happens to me. But I refuse to be reduced by it."

– From Letter to My Daughter, Random House, 2008.

Barack Obama. Quote: "Our destiny is not written for us but by us."

– 2009 Inaugural Address, January 20, 2009.

Mahatma Gandhi. Quote: "Happiness is when what you think, what you say, and what you do are in harmony."

Long Walk to Freedom: The Autobiography of Nelson Mandela. Little, Brown and Company, 1994.

Oprah Winfrey – Public interviews and speeches, including SuperSoul Sunday (OWN Network).

The Holy Bible, 1 John 1:9 (King James Version).

Johns Hopkins Medicine – The Healing Power of Forgiveness. <u>https://www.hopkinsmedicine.org</u>

The Autobiography of Malcolm X as told to Alex Haley. Ballantine Books, 1965.

The Master Plan: My Journey from Life in Prison to a Life of Purpose by Chris Wilson with Bret Witter. G.P. Putnam's Sons, 2019.

The Holy Bible, Proverbs 29:18 (King James Version).

Senghor, S. (2016). Writing my wrongs: Life, death, and redemption in an American prison. Convergent Books.

Centers for Disease Control and Prevention (CDC). "Physical Activity and Health." *CDC.gov*, 2022. https://www.cdc.gov/physicalactivity/basics/pa-health/index.htm

Brown-Long, Cyntoia. *Free Cyntoia: My Search for Redemption in the American Prison System.* Atria Books, 2019.

Tolle, Eckhart. *The Power of Now.* New World Library, 1999.

Moore, Thomas. *Care of the Soul.* HarperPerennial, 1994.

Williamson, Marianne. *A Return to Love.* HarperOne, 1992.

Dispenza, Joe. *Becoming Supernatural.* Hay House, 2017.

Carroll, Curtis "Wall Street". Interviews and media appearances via *TED Talks* and *The Marshall Project*

Brown, Brené. *Daring Greatly*. Gotham Books, 2012.

Cloud, Henry & Townsend, John. *Boundaries: When to Say Yes, How to Say No*. Zondervan, 1992.

"The Power of Mentorship and Peer Support in Reentry," Urban Institute

Sarah's story adapted from testimonials compiled by *A New Way of Life Reentry Project*

Jesse Crosson / Second Chancer Foundation – secondchancer.org

The Marshall Project – "Life After Prison" Series

Urban Institute – "Returning Home" Reentry Studies

Defy Ventures – Post-release entrepreneurship and mentoring

The Fortune Society – Reentry services and housing

U.S. Dept. of Education – Resources on Pell Grants for formerly incarcerated individuals

YouTube Learning / Coursera / Khan Academy – Free skill development platforms

www.ingramcontent.com/pod-product-compliance
Lightning Source LLC
Chambersburg PA
CBHW070128030426
42335CB00016B/2300